SHOWBUS
THE WOBURN AND DUXFORD YEARS

GARY SEAMARKS

AMBERLEY

First published 2020

Amberley Publishing
The Hill, Stroud
Gloucestershire, GL5 4EP

www.amberley-books.com

British Library Cataloguing in Publication Data.
A catalogue record for this book is available from the British Library.

ISBN 978 1 4456 9352 1 (print)
ISBN 978 1 4456 9353 8 (ebook)

Typeset in 11pt on 14pt Sabon.
Typesetting by Aura Technology and Software Services, India.
Printed in the UK.

Introduction

Throughout its almost fifty-year history, the annual Showbus Rally has been held at various sites, firstly around the Hillingdon area, and more recently on the Leicestershire/Derbyshire border at Donnington. The majority, though, were hosted by two very differing sites north of London: Woburn Abbey in Bedfordshire between 1982 and 1992, and across the border at Duxford IWM near Cambridge between 1993 and 2012, then again in 2014 before a one-off at Woburn in 2015. The thirty-three years between the first and last of these events, which are illustrated in this publication, were to see massive changes in the UK bus and coach industry, with many big names at the 1982 event no longer on the scene in 2015.

1982 had seen Tottenham Hotspur win the FA Cup and Liverpool were League Champions, with Kevin Keegan top goal-scorer. Channel 4 would launch a few weeks later, and Margaret Thatcher was the Prime Minster. Perhaps most apt was the fact that Survivor's 'Eye of the Tiger' would knock 'Come on Eileen' by Dexy's Midnight Runners off the top of the pop charts on the rally weekend; the event was sponsored by Leyland, whose Tiger chassis had been designed with an eye to the UK coach market, with the real beasts across the park in the vast Wild Animal Kingdom. Red Rover provided tours of the Wild Animal Kingdom, while connections from London were provided by Leyland Bendibuses that connected with trains at Aylesbury station. The abbey grounds were to provide a wonderful setting on a good day but were unsuitable for heavy vehicles in wet weather, which sadly appeared too often.

The start of the 1980s had seen London Transport dominate the capital, with Municipals and PTEs running the routes in many major towns and cities routes. The National Bus Company was the main rural provider and in addition had an unchallenged monopoly in many other urban areas. Deregulation would change the industry in 1986, along with privatisation, which, by the late 1980s, had seen almost all the former NBC fleets sold off, with familiar vehicles appearing in very unfamiliar liveries. Unfamiliar operators gained London tenders, all of which brought interest to the event. For 1988 the rally moved from the traditional September slot to early July but the following year it reverted back to September. This was also the year that the first Stagecoach-liveried buses appeared at the rally, with the United Counties fleet just up the road in Beds and Northants part of the growing Stagecoach empire. Into the 1990s and it was the end for London Transport, by now called London Buses, as it was split up ready for privatisation. Some customised liveries were appearing in the capital and at Showbus.

Sadly for Woburn, the weather in the end proved the winner, with the 1992 show almost washed out by floods; last-minute changes split the rally site, with many vehicles located at a second site near the safari park, with buses carrying visitors between the two sites. Enough was enough and for 1993 a new location was found, across to the east at the Imperial War Museum at Duxford, just south of Cambridge, where much more hardstanding was provided. Coupled with the aircraft and other military history, which provided a secondary attraction as well as somewhere to shelter if the weather turned, this meant the 1993 event was the first to achieve 300 entries. With more modern vehicles seeming to outnumber the preserved vehicles, the event was becoming a showcase for the new major groups to show off their new products and liveries. An added bonus for some coach operators at Duxford was that they were used to run excursions to the rally. One area that seemed to grow over the course of the Duxford era was the sale of model buses, with EFE bringing what seemed like an ever-growing marquee for its display; they were the first sponsors of the rally in 1994 and each year brought more and more stalls competing in the market. Other major players in the industry were also involved in sponsorship over the years, including Scania, whose headquarters at Milton Keynes was just up the road from Woburn. Badgerline/First and then Go-Ahead sponsored the plaques for many years, with Arriva later becoming very supporting. The event grew year on year, attracting entries from across the country and, in some cases, beyond.

The year 2001 had seen the terror attacks of 9/11 in the US a few days prior to the event; in addition, a fuel tanker drivers' dispute just before the event, coupled with foot-and-mouth disease, had a dramatic effect on the UK countryside where many preserved buses were stored; the event, though, went ahead. In 2002 the Queen's Golden Jubilee produced several entries in Jubilee-styled liveries and the vehicle entries topped 400 for the first time. Anniversaries were celebrated most years, including 2004 – the Routemaster's fiftieth anniversary – and 2007 – Plaxton's centenary. For 2011 the main sponsor became TTCDiecast; the company's stall sold models by the thousand, it seemed. 2012 was a big year for the UK with the Diamond Jubilee of the

Queen and the Summer Olympics in London. A special 'Gold Run' from Royston was arranged to show a timeline of development from 1952 to 2012, several of which were in Jubilee liveries for what became the fortieth Showbus.

A change of venue in 2013 would see the event move to near Stratford-upon-Avon before returning to Duxford in 2014 for the final time, where the international theme was lived up to with buses that had worked on all five continents appearing, even if one was an RT that had been used as a tourist bus in the United States. The 2015 event was a return to Woburn, which sadly, due to external factors, did not live up to expectations, but that is not the subject of this publication. However, an amazing selection of pre-Second World War buses was assembled alongside the latest offerings from a wide range of operators, which presented a vastly changed picture from 1982.

The thirty-three years between the first and last events at these two venues had seen changes nobody could have foreseen in 1982, when Leyland dominated the industry with its National, and Olympians, many bodied by ECW at Lowestoft for NBC and PTE fleets that would be absorbed into the big five of Arriva, First, Go-Ahead, National Express and Stagecoach, the latter in 1982 a small Perth-based independent. Destination blinds and ticket machines that were, in the main, worked by a small handle gave way to electronic versions. The event itself had gone online, with visitors aware of the entrants before the day, but programmes were still much sought-after, though their style and quality changed regularly and progressed from an A5 size to the later standard A4 format, including many articles on the modern bus scene as well as lists of the growing number of vehicles entered as the popularity of the event grew. To many, that Sunday in September is Showbus Sunday. The advent of digital photography now sees many visitors taking hundreds of images, whereas back in 1982 every photo taken was at a financial cost which sadly limited the amount taken.

I have tried to select a cross-section of what has appeared at the two locations over this period, grouped loosely into batches, but with such a cross-section appearing, some interesting vehicles will have been missed out, for which I apologise. But working on 300 buses per event over thirty-three years, that's an incredible number of vehicles that have been displayed for the benefit of others. All photos are from my own collection and those from before 2006 are 35 mm; if only digital had been around in 1982. This book has no connection with the event and just contains some of my memories from the events.

Gary Seamarks
November 2019

Acknowledgments

Special thanks must go to those who have organised this popular event over such a long period of time. Thanks also go to those who brought their vehicles – some over long distances – to the event; for many the trip was long and slow and meant at least one night away from home. Much information has been obtained from old event programs, as well as the PSV Circle and various websites, to which thanks are offered. Finally, thanks to those who have purchased this publication.

Delaine of Bourne has been a loyal supporter of the event, displaying both new and older vehicles. For 2010 the company entered RCT3, one of only two double-decker bodies built by Yeates, both of which were built on Leyland PD3/1 chassis for Delaine in 1960. This became the first vehicle preserved by the company when withdrawn in 1979. It's being followed onto the site by SF55 HHB, a Wright-bodied Volvo B7RLE that had recently been acquired.

Delivered to Stagecoach London as a replacement for the Trident lost in the London terror attacks of 7 July 2005, this was the first E400, 19000 (LX55 HGC), with suitable wording in memory of those sadly no longer with us as well as those whose lives were changed forever on that day. It is seen in 2015.

Travel West Midlands invested in a large quantity of low-floor double-deckers, with over 350 in service by late 2002, including a batch of 100 Tridents with Alexander ALX400 bodies in 1999, of which 4128 (Y719 TOH) was painted up for the 2002 Golden Jubilee. It's seen here arriving on site.

Delivered new to Grey-Green for the 24 were a batch of Volvo Citybus/Alexander including VA157 (H157 XYU), which by 2002 had become part of Arriva's London operation and was selected for the Jubilee treatment, sponsored by various companies, in this case Surf.

The first Woburn of 1982 was in the thirtieth year of HM Queen Elizabeth's reign. For her fiftieth year, in 2002, many operators celebrated with golden liveries. Stagecoach East's 453 (JAH 553D), an ECW-bodied Bristol FLF that had been new to Eastern Counties, was painted in revised colours of the then new Stagecoach livery.

The only RT to be painted for the 2002 Golden Jubilee was RT4712 (NXP 997), which had been new in 1954 and is now part of the London Transport Museum fleet, allocated to the Arriva London fleet but not used in normal service. The livery was retained after the event, as seen on RT4712's arrival at Duxford in 2003.

Fast-forward ten years to the sixtieth and we see Stagecoach South's Scania 15586 (GX59 JYT) decorated with bunting on a slightly revised livery that omitted the orange stripes. Unlike the silver and golden jubilees, fewer buses wore diamond jubilee liveries. It is seen in 2012.

Another bus decorated for the Diamond Jubilee in 2012. East Yorkshire applied this split livery to 713 (YX06 CXO), a Volvo B7TL with Wright bodywork, which participated in the Gold Run of sixty vehicles from nearby Royston, unlike other years where the nearby park and rides were used.

Although new as a true London bus, the Routemaster found a new lease of life on the deregulation of bus services in 1986, with many heading to Scotland. Newly formed Strathtay Scottish took batches for both Perth and Dundee. SR21 (VLT 26) has made the long trip south for the Woburn event in July 1988.

Routemasters were never operated by Great Yarmouth Borough Transport, but FirstGroup did operate a small batch in the Norfolk resort on a coastal route that connected various holiday resort villages to the town. RML2717 (SMK 717F) shows its colours at Duxford in 2007.

Leyland developed an in-house double-decker, code name B15, with integral Park Royal bodywork in the mid-1970s. NHG 732P had been one of three development vehicles, all dual-doored, and later passed to Gagg's of Bunny (Notts) and was rebuilt to single-door layout. It is seen in 1989.

Outside of London there were few takers for the B15, which had been renamed the Titan. West Midlands PTE ordered eighty but only took five, all single-doored examples, in 1978/9, including 7003 (WDA 3T). A subsequent order was cancelled and the five were soon sold to London, for use mainly as private hire vehicles with coach seating. It is seen in 1989.

Greater Manchester had ordered a batch of 190 Titans but in the event only took fifteen, which were sold as surplus at deregulation. South Midland at Witney purchased a batch of six for the Bicester–Oxford service, where the full height was no issue. They were all painted in the same livery worn by 706 (GNF 11V), seen arriving at Woburn in 1988.

Although the initial 250 Titans for London were built at Park Royal in West London, production switched in 1981 to Cumbria, where NUW 598Y had been built as London's T598. After its passenger-carrying days were over, Ensignbus converted it into a mobile police station in 2000 for Cambridgeshire Police and it served the force for almost ten years. It is seen in 2007.

Leaving Woburn in 1989, this is RT1 (EYK 396). But in effect it is not the original RT1, which was a 1938 AEC Regent III fitted with the body off TD111 for a few months before this LTPB body was fitted in 1939. Later, after passing through LT's overhaul, the body returned to service on 1949 chassis. After its London days were over the bus would spend three years in the United States between 1983 and 1986.

The London Transport area suffered, like others, from its fair share of low bridges as the railway companies had never envisaged double-decker buses. For this reason, the RLH class of seventy-six AEC Regent IIIs with low-height Weymann bodies were purchased between 1950 and 1952. RLH32 (MXX 232) is seen in Samuel Ledgard livery, although it was never part of that fleet. It is seen in 2015.

With over 4,800 RT buses built for London, it's of no surprise that many were later preserved. Red RT3251 (LLU 610) of 1950 was new to the country fleet in green and transferred back from London Country in 1972, while green RT4494 (OLD714) of 1954 was new as a Green Line vehicle at Grays. They are both fitted with Weymann bodies and are seen in 2006.

While the last of the RT family were being built, London Transport were busy designing and building its replacement, the Routemaster. RM1 (SLT56) was new in 1954 and by 1957 was joined by three other prototype vehicles. It was not until 1989 that it was donated to the LT Collection, appearing on many last days of RM routes in London, and in 2004 appearing at Duxford.

London Transport had offloaded its country operations to NBC in 1970 as London Country Bus Services. It was all change again in 1986 when LCBS were split into four, with more fragmentation to follow. New to LCBS as LR44 (A144 DPE), this Roe-bodied Olympian was, by 1989, based at the Harlow garage of Sovereign Bus and had recently been painted in their Townlink livery.

Kentish Bus had seen the chance to pick up LRT work and acquired three routes into the heart of London in 1990, for which forty-three Leyland Olympians with Northern Counties bodies were purchased. 530 (G530 VBB) is seen leaving Woburn in 1990 for its Leyton depot. Kentish Bus would later fall under Arriva ownership.

Seen when almost new, at Duxford in 1997, this is Metrobus 841 (R841 MFR), one of fifteen Volvo Olympians with East Lancs Pyoneer bodies for the recently won LRT route 64 between Thornton Heath and New Addington. It would serve its first five years of service there before the contracts stated that all London buses had to be red.

Backing the bid in 2004, this was Stagecoach London Trident 18209 (LX04 FWV). The country would have to wait until July 2005 to find out that the host city for the 2012 Olympics and Paralympics would be London, which would generate much income for Stagecoach and other operators from far and wide, transporting hundreds of thousands of people to various locations across London and beyond.

While many dual-door buses had been used in London, V3 (A103 SUU) would remain unique. One of three Volvo Ailsas delivered in 1984 with Alexander RV bodywork, it would feature twin staircases with the second door positioned at the rear. Almost thirty years later the LT class would be built to a very similar layout and would also be designed for a crew of two. V3 is seen here in 2007.

LT7 was the first of the LT class to appear at Showbus, still bearing the registration LT12 GHT at the 2012 event; this would later change to LTZ 1007. The first eight were trailed on Arriva's 38 route between Clapton Pond and Victoria during 2012. For the record, LT256 appeared at the 2014 event, while LT190 went to Woburn in 2015.

Former London STL1470 (CXX 457), a 1936 AEC Regent with Weymann body, was converted at Aldenham in 1953 into a tree lopper with a fold-down door to aid with removal of cuttings. It was used at Hemel Hempstead and St Albans garages until 1963, back when bus companies would trim trees that were likely to cause damage to their vehicles.

Over the years, London has operated examples of what could be classed 'next generation' buses. With a hint of steam rising from the rear roofbox, ESQ64993 (LK53 MBV) was one of a batch of three Hydrogen fuel cell powered Mercedes Citaros that were allocated to First for test purposes. It is seen here in 2004.

While others saw the advantages of having doors towards the front on half-cab buses, London stuck with the open platform for all of its Routemasters. The exceptions were the Green Line coach version and RMF1254 (254 CLT), which appeared at the 1962 Commercial Motor Show before spending the next four years on demonstration loans or in store before sale to Northern General. It operated there alongside fifty similar vehicles bought new and is seen here in 2014.

Alongside operators showing off new vehicles in 1984, London Buses brought RM1288 (288 CLT), a modified Routemaster, to the event. It was destined for China in an attempt to sell redundant RMs that still had plenty of life left. In the event, it remained unique.

Perhaps one of Woburn's best assets was the backdrops for photographing the arrival of vehicles, as shown here in 1984 with RF676 (NLE 676), an AEC Regal with Metro-Cammell bodywork of 1953. The RF class worked across most of the former London Transport sphere of operation for many years, with the last examples withdrawn in 1979.

Although I attended all the Woburn events, it was not until 1984 that I purchased my first 35mm camera, and as such I only have limited images from 1982/3. Former London Country XF3 (CUV 53C), a Fleetline with Park Royal bodywork, was photographed in 1983 on a seemingly deserted field.

London Country continued to buy from AEC/Park Royal in the early years, including a batch of ninety Reliances with dual-purpose bodies, such as RP21 (JPA 121K), which helped modernise the Green Line network by removing the aging RF fleet that had been inherited from London Transport. RP21 is seen here in 2006.

London Country took five AEC Reliances with Plaxton coach bodies, with a one-piece door, in 1973. Although new in plain white National livery, they were allocated across the network for use on private hire work initially. They did not carry fleet numbers until 1975 and were simply referred to by registration number. All five lasted until the breakup of LC in 1986. SPK 203M would later be acquired by the London Bus Preservation Trust and restored to 1977 Green Line livery. It is seen here in 2014.

The Green Line routes received Leyland Tigers with Plaxton Paramount bodies from late 1983. These were leased and once disposed of, they appeared across the country. Former TP3 (A103 EPA) was entered into the Duxford event of 1995 by its new owner, Thamesdown, and is seen alongside a next generation Green Line Plaxton Paramount of Luton & District, who had taken over from the former St Albans garage on routes to Luton Airport.

Competition had seen the end of many Green Line routes from the late 1980s and by 2008 just a few key routes survived, mostly to the north and west of London. Arriva the Shires had invested in a batch of fifteen tri-axle Van Hool T917s in 2008/9, mostly for the Luton Airport–London route, but 4376 (YJ58 FJV) was one of a handful later based at Hemel for route 758 to London and it is seen here in 2014.

Although Arriva were a major player in the Green Line network, First Berkshire retained a route to the west of London that served the Legoland theme park, which generated decent loadings, and so First purchased three higher-spec Volvo B9TLs with sixty-five-seat Wright bodies, including 37276 (LK58 EDL), which is seen here in 2008. These were the first double-deckers for Green Line since some Olympians in the 1980s.

Stagecoach's Oxford Tube operates a 24/7 service into London. During 2009 the entire allocation of Neoplan Skyliners were replaced with twenty-six new Van Hool low-floor double-deck coaches, including 50223 (OU59 AUW), which had still to enter service on the route. The batch were replaced in 2014 by similar new vehicles.

During the early 1980s Southend Transport had built up a considerable coach fleet for its highly successful London services. In 1983 they purchased three Van Hool TD824 Astromegas that seated eighty-four for this flagship route. Two more followed in late 1985. Former 245 (JEV 245Y) is now preserved by Ensignbus and is seen here in 2015.

Several NBC fleets built up considerable networks of commuter coaches travelling into London in the early 1980s, attracting passengers disillusioned by disruptions to rail travel. Maidstone & District branded their services under the Invictaway branding. Impressive additions were made to the fleet by ECW-bodied long wheelbase Leyland Olympians such as the now preserved 5442 (GKE 442Y), seen in 2011.

One of the pioneers of double-deck coaches in the UK was Standerwick. The opening of the motorway network led to a batch of Atlanteans in the early 1960s which were followed by a batch of thirty Bristol VRLs with sixty-seat ECW bodies a decade later, including 60 (LRN 60J), seen here in 2010. They were withdrawn after an accident on the M1 which was caused by outside factors.

Deregulated coach services in the UK from the early 1980s brought about an upsurge in competition for National Express from several operators who were using double-deck coaches. NX approached MCW, who in effect reworked a Hong Kong design to produce the Metroliner, which both NX and the Scottish Bus Group took. They were perhaps not the ideal choice and many were soon disposed of, including C647 FTT, which by 1993 had passed to Hulme Hall Coaches from Manchester.

On-a-Mission Coaches from near Milton Keynes brought MK56 DON, a rather high-spec Ayats Bravo, to the Duxford event of 2008. It was sporting lettering for its role as the MK Dons' first team transport that featured tables and an upstairs kitchen area. Regretfully, a couple of years later it was mission over and no more running wild when the company closed down.

Beds in Beds could be the caption from Woburn 2015 with Stagecoach Scotland West 50313 (YJ64 AUR) heading into the event. The big Van Hool TDX29 with seating for just fifty-five was one of the fleet of vehicles that were quickly converted into sleeping coaches for the overnight London–Scotland routes.

The Bedford VAL had been introduced in the 1960s to the then 36-foot maximum length with a 'Chinese 6' wheel plan of twin steering axles; low-profile wheels were also fitted. EHL 472D, with a Plaxton Panorama body, was new to West Riding in 1966 and is seen here in 1987. Most VALs were fitted with Leyland 0.400 or 0.470 engines.

Another Bedford VAL that appeared at the event was ORU 581G, in 1993. By then it was a non-PSV, having started life with Hants & Dorset in 1969 for its Shamrock & Rambler operation. The Duple Viceroy body features opening windows for ventilation.

Some of the last coaches delivered to the former National Bus Company were a batch of six Duple 425s with seating for fifty-seven, new to Alder Valley South for Londonlinks routes. These included E208 EPB, which appeared at the 2011 event along with several others of the type owned by Trekkers of Harlow.

East Kent had taken both styles of MCW Metroliner single-deck coach, mostly for its share of National Holidays work initially. 8855 (E855 UKR) is seen at the 2004 event, when it was owned by Provence Private Hire of St Albans, Hertfordshire, and retains its blue destination blinds from its East Kent days.

Lothian had received two early Leyland Olympians in 1982 Alexander bodies. 667 (GSC 667X), which is now retained in the Lothian Heritage fleet, made the long trip to Duxford in 2000. It would be 1988 before the next Alexander-bodied examples appeared, with ECW supplying 128 between late 1982 and early 1986.

Another Lothian bus to appear was GSX 121N, in 2003, one of a batch of ten Bedford YRTs with Alexander Y-type bodies delivered in 1974 for tour and coaching work. They were all downgraded to bus service work after just one season, and GSX 121N was later transferred to the heritage fleet.

Leyland's answer to the Volvo Citybus was the Lion, introduced in 1986. Eastern Scottish ZLL177 (C177 VSF) was one of a batch used in conjunction with the 1986 Commonwealth Games held in Edinburgh. It is seen at Woburn with the games' logos still evident on its Alexander body. In the event only thirty-two Lions were built.

The Scottish Bus Group operated many services across the border, with London a major terminal for both day and night routes. Alexander's M-type body was designed for these services, resembling the famous Greyhound coaches in the USA, with most mounted on Bristol REMH or Leyland Leopard chassis. This one, new to Eastern Scottish, was a Seddon Pennine XS750 (MSF 750P) – only six of this combination were built – and carries the distinctive livery of the 1970s when seen in 2009.

Unlike the standardised liveries applied by the National Bus Company, the Scottish Bus Group retained individual liveries for each fleet. Alexander (Northern) retained its traditional yellow livery, as seen on NPE102 (JSA 102V), a Leyland Leopard with Alexander AT body, a type used by many SBG fleets on longer inter-urban routes.

Stagecoach inherited many longer-distance routes in Scotland which relied on coaches. The typical vehicles purchased to upgrade these were Volvo B10Ms with Plaxton Interurban bodies such as 636 (R636 RSE) of the Northern Bluebird fleet, which also displays the royal warrant, and had made the trip south in 1998.

Vehicles under restoration have often appeared at the event. Seen at Duxford in 2005, this is L407 (SGD 407), a 1960 Leyland PD3/2 with seventy-two-seat Alexander bodywork that was part way through being returned to the Glasgow Corporation livery that it carried when new.

While many Ailsas were new to Scottish fleets, PSJ 825R was one of only two that carried the Van Hool McArdle body. Both were destined for the A1 service fleet in Ayrshire. Although built as dual-doored, rebuilding to single door had been undertaken by a subsequent owner. It is seen here in 2005.

BEA took new buses for its transfer work in 1966, turning to the Routemaster for its needs. In total sixty-five were taken and were capable of 70 mph for the motorway section along the newly opened M4; for passengers' luggage, a total of eighty-eight trailers were built by Marshalls and attached to the rear. As the service was wound down between 1975 and 1979, the vehicles passed to LT as the RMA class with many used as trainers. The first of the batch, KGJ 601D, arrives at Duxford in 2009 in as-new livery.

With private car ownership rising, the need for airport buses changed, with car park transfers and internal shuttles becoming more relevant. Posed in 2007 by the restored BAC-111 at Duxford is British Airways Citaro BU07 KXY. Of note are the offside door and the roof-mounted light for airside operation.

BEA had taken delivery of sixty-five AEC Regal IVs in 1953 to transport passengers between their West London Air Terminal and Heathrow Airport; they were operated and maintained by LT. The raised seating at the rear of the Park Royal body allowed extra luggage space for these duties. MLL740 would be the last of the type in service with BEA, in 1973; here in 2010 it stands alongside RF4 (LUC 204), one of the twenty-five private hire RFs, new in 1951.

BOAC had taken delivery of fifteen Roe-bodied Atlanteans in late 1966 for use on its connecting service between Central London and Heathrow, with additional luggage space at the rear of the lower deck, accessed by the door behind the rear axle, which restricted the seating to thirty-eight over sixteen. LYF 307D is seen at the 2011 event alongside Duxford's ex-BOAC VC10.

New to Westcliff-on-Sea MS, AJN 825 was a Bristol K5G that later became part of the Eastern National fleet. Delivered in 1939, this pre-Second World War bus was fitted with an ECW L27/26R configured body, and was a regular sight at rallies in this era. It is seen here in 1989.

Former Eastern National VNO 859, a Bristol KSW5G, leaves the 1989 event to head home through Woburn village. New in 1953, its ECW body seated fifty-five and featured upper-deck four-abreast seating and a sunken offside gangway, much hated by passengers and conductors alike.

Reading had taken delivery in 1957 of four low-height AEC Regent IIIs with Park Royal bodies seating twenty-seven over twenty-six. 4 (MRD 147) was still on fleet strength in 1984 when it attended the event with new 147 (B147 EDP), a Metrobus Mk II that was branded for the company's Goldline operation.

When NEH 453 was delivered to Potteries in 1949, it was fitted with a Weymann B35F body which was later replaced by this low-height Northern Counties body in the mid-1950s. To add to the interest, the chassis is a Leyland Titan OPD2/1, which meant it was originally built for export. It is seen here in 2014.

The East Kent fleet contained many AEC/Park Royal vehicles in the early 1960s. PFN 874 was one of thirty-nine similar AEC Regent Vs delivered in 1958/9, complete with full front and sliding door, and is seen here in 1984. The FN registration mark was carried by many vehicles in this fleet, in which fleet numbering was not introduced until the 1970s.

The Southdown Queen Mary was a popular visitor at many of the events. In this busy scene from 1991 can be seen 260 (BUF 260C), one of the 1965 intake of these Leyland PD3/4s with Northern Counties bodies that formed a major part of the Southdown fleet for many years, which also included some convertible to open-top.

One of very few full-front low-height buses built was Barton's 861 (861 HAL), new in 1961 and seen here in 1985. The stylish Northern Counties body, which seated sixty-eight, was fitted to a Dennis Loline chassis. The combination achieved a height of just 12 feet 6 inches, almost 2 feet below a highbridge design of the same era.

A body configuration unique to Bournemouth is seen on KEL131, a 1950 Leyland Titan PD2/3 with Weymann body that featured an open platform for boarding and a forward exit protected by folding doors. Internally, two sets of staircases were fitted. A similar arrangement existed in the trolleybuses within the fleet. KEL131 is seen in 1985.

What had begun life as a Bristol LH with ECW body, Hants & Dorset 3516 (NLJ 516M) had been transformed in 1982 into a somewhat oversized charabanc for the Shamrock & Rambler fleet in Bournemouth. In 1984 it had made the trip to a sunny Woburn Abbey, where it is seen arriving, followed by a former Southend Leyland Titan.

A Leyland PD3/1 with Metro-Cammell bodywork, XRY 202 was new to Leicester in 1959. Along with several others, it would later pass to Guard's of London, who had it rebuilt to resemble a mock vintage bus complete with open staircase for a London sightseeing tour in the mid-1970s. It is seen here in 1986.

What had started life as a standard London Fleetline, DMS1515 (THM 515M) was rebuilt in 1991 as the part-DMS, part-Underground train Class 321 to promote the travelcard ticket for use in London. Owned by London Underground, it toured many events in the capital during the early 1990s but was then off the scene for many years. Now preserved, it attended Showbus in 2012.

Only six of these Quest B80s with Locomotors bodies were built, all for Merseyside PTE, where they had a short working life. By Showbus 1990, B930 KWM was working in Watford for Lucky Bus. As can be seen, the weather has taken a turn for the worse and many people seem to be making a speedy exit.

A Leyland development vehicle that acquired a Q plate was Q723 GHG, a rear-engined Leyland Tiger with an ECW body seating fifty-one that had been built as an experimental vehicle in 1985, but not registered until 1991, and was perhaps the last ECW to be registered. It was purchased by OK Motor Services, who brought it down to Duxford in 1995.

Buses bearing a Q plate were almost guaranteed to be worth a second look. This shot from 1984 sees what would be Q246 FVT of Stevenson's Spath arriving at Woburn. Having been new in 1979 as chassis B45.01 and ECW body EX14, it would not be until November 1984 that it would be registered, hence the Q plate. Of note is the lower front panel, which is of Bristol VR origin, a feature that would appear on several other Olympians later in their lives.

Looking very much like it had been converted from a double-decker, 40 (GEX 740F) was one of three similar Leyland Atlanteans with thirty-nine-seat Marshall bodywork that were operated by Great Yarmouth, prior to the operator opting for the AEC Swift for its single-decker requirements. It is seen here in 1985.

Converted to single deck after an accident with a low bridge in 1994, Travel West Midlands 6956 (WDA 956T) was a MCW-bodied Leyland Fleetline. The rebuilding featured a new front dome and roof. Although more conversions were planned, it was to remain unique and is seen here at Duxford in 2010, being parked next to a Darlington Roe-bodied single deck Fleetline No. 27 (VHN 527G).

With the close proximity to its Milton Keynes offices, several Scania demonstrators appeared at the Woburn event. For 1989 it was G113 SKX, an Alexander PS-bodied N113CRB, that was chosen. This would later see service with Busways in Newcastle.

Demonstration coaches were a key feature of the Leyland sales campaign. In 1985 this Tiger with Plaxton Paramount body was an entry. B254 AMG featured a manual gearbox, which was preferred by many smaller independent coach fleets. The high-floor Paramount body seated fifty-one and also had a toilet fitted.

Perhaps one of the most unusual new vehicles to be shown at Showbus was this 1971-built Ford R192 with Duple Viceroy body that had sat in a dealer's premises for forty years until acquired by Sharpe's of Nottingham for its heritage fleet. It's seen in 2014, still unregistered.

Plaxton's have for many years been one of the major sponsors of the event, bringing their latest models to the show. For the 2009 event this Elite on a tri-axle Volvo B12B chassis was placed centre stage with another British classic, the VC10, for company.

Midland Red were keen early users of the M1 when it opened in 1959 with no speed limits imposed. At that time Midland Red were still building their own vehicles, badged as BMMO, and the C5 was introduced for such workings. 4819 (819 HHA) shows the initial livery of these vehicles when new in 1961, although it lasted until 1971. Records show the vehicle as only used during the summer months and placed in store each winter. It is seen here in 1987.

The early 1980s had seen the first signs of the break-up of the NBC fleets with several of the major fleets split into smaller units. Midland Fox, based in Leicester, brought this Olympian/ECW (A508 EJF) to Woburn in 1984 in their impressive livery. This was one of the first double-deckers bought new by the company.

The Midland Red area encompassed much of the Midlands and beyond, with many busy routes requiring double-deckers. 5424 (EHA 424D) was one of almost 350 BMMO D9 types produced between 1959 and 1966 and which took advantage of the 30-foot maximum length permitted then for double-deckers. It is seen here in 2010. Also featuring a semi-automatic gearbox, the D9 would be the last BMMO double-decker introduced.

Privatisation of the former NBC fleets split up the former Midland Red empire forever. Later, all would be owned by the big groups, either Stagecoach (South), Firstbus (West) or Arriva (Fox and North). 4720 (PX52 XBH), an East Lancs-bodied DAF SB250, shows the new era at a wet Duxford in 2002 in the company of PWE 534R, an Alexander-bodied Fleetline that Fox acquired from South Yorkshire.

Oxford was one of the National Bus Company fleets that was split in 1983, with the country depots being split off to form South Midland. Part of a mixed fleet that contained Fleetlines, VRs and REs in the main, Bristol VR TBW 451P shows the ORBITER livery for services to the west of Oxford that connected at Gloucester Green with Oxford Bus routes to London. It is seen here in 1985.

Like many other cities, Oxford suffers from traffic congestion and was keen to develop a Park & Ride network, which does help the situation. Newly delivered in 1988 were five dual-door Alexander RL-bodied Olympians for such work, for example 228 (E228 CFC), seen at the event that was held in July that year.

Oxford Bus had taken a batch of Leyland Titans cascaded from London in the early 1990s. They were numbered in the 9xx series, which was reserved for vehicles unable to fit under the station bridge. 975 (A869 SUL) is seen at Duxford in 2007 while owned by Wootten's of Amersham, but retaining its Oxford Bus livery.

1987 had seen the arrival in Oxford of Thames Transit, who initially ran high frequency minibus routes, alongside the Tube services to London. This is Mellor-bodied Ford Transit D122 PTT. Thames Transit later merged with South Midland and were finally sold to Stagecoach, in whose ownership D122 PTT was in by 1998.

Cambus had been formed in September 1984 when the Cambridgeshire section of Eastern Counties and Newmarket depot were split off. Although almost all the fleet were suitable for one-person operation, BNG 886B, a 1963 Bristol FS6G with ECW body, had found its way into the fleet and by the time of Showbus 1987 it was painted into a version of the then current livery.

A short-lived City Sightseeing route from Cambridge to the Duxford site was contracted to Stagecoach. Dart 33305 (AE51 VFX) had been new to Cavalier (Long Sutton), arriving when that fleet was purchased in 2008 and later going on to non-PSV duties within the fleet. It is seen here in 2011.

Like many NBC fleets, Cambus relied heavily on the Bristol VR for its trunk routes through the 1980s. New to Eastern Counties, VR246 (KVF 246V) was part of the initial Cambus fleet. Here it's seen in 1986, but thirty years later I would catch up with it in the Highlands as a site office.

Cambridge once had a strong independent bus scene, with Whippet, Premier Travel and Burwell & District running into the university city. 9DER was the first Willowbrook-bodied Fleetline, built and supplied in 1963 to Burwell & District, where it lasted until they ceased in 1979. Although preserved for many years, severe corrosion later saw it reduced to just the front end, retained in a museum. It is seen here in 1985.

During the 1970s the National Bus Company had purchased batches of lightweight buses in an attempt to cut down on running costs. The nearby United Counties fleet had taken over sixty Willowbrook-bodied Bedfords in 1974–6 and in 1977 received ten Ford R1014s with Duple Dominant forty-three-seat bodies, including 59 (OVV 59R). Neither type lasted more than seven years in the fleet, with many snapped up by independent operators. By 2010 the former 59 had been restored to 'as new' condition.

United Counties were the local NBC subsidiary to Woburn in 1985. In that year, this Bristol KS5G/ECW (FRP692) is seen arriving at the event with blinds set for the 141 route, which originated in St Ives, travelling via Huntingdon and Bedford (where a change of buses was always required) before heading to Aylesbury.

United Counties had developed a thriving private hire business in the early 1980s that included work into mainland Europe. In late 1983 the company invested in three upmarket Leyland Tigers with Plaxton Paramount bodies. They all had selective issue registrations, as seen on 82 (82 LUP) at Woburn in 1985. On the split of the company, each of the new units was allocated one coach.

A long-term regular attendee at Showbus, F110 NES was the unique 110-seat tri-axle Olympian. Although it spent almost twenty-five years at Bedford between 1992 and 2017, the honour of taking 'Nessie' to the event first fell to East Midland's Mansfield depot, in 1990. After retirement, it became part of the group's heritage fleet.

Split from United Counties in 1985, Luton & District later became a major part of Arriva the Shires. In 2013 they had taken delivery of a batch of electric Streetlite DFs for a cross-town route in Milton Keynes, from where 5007 (KP63 TEU) has made the short trip to Woburn in 2015.

Four upmarket Citaros with 2 + 1 leather seating were delivered new to MK Metro in 2009 for park and ride duties to MK Coachway, located by the M1. 3926 (BG59 FCV) is seen at the 2010 event. Until 1986 the Milton Keynes operation had been part of United Counties, but in 2006 it would become part of Arriva the Shires.

Southdown amassed a large fleet of Leyland Leopards during the 1960s and 1970s, with bodywork by Plaxton, Duple, Marshall, Harrington and Willowbrook. However, they only took twenty built by Northern Counties with dual-purpose bodywork, in 1969, as 460–79 (PUF 160–79H). Preserved 465 appeared at Woburn in 2002 in NBC dual-purpose livery.

Southdown took delivery of its first Volvos in 1989, at the time of the sale to Stagecoach. These were a batch of twelve Northern Counties B10M-50s with coach seating. 302 (F302 MYJ) is seen arriving at Duxford in 1995, celebrating the ninetieth anniversary of the company in the privatisation livery that had been succeeded by Stagecoach stripes.

Several Routemasters have been sold for non-PSV use as mobile bars, including the former RCL2240 (CUV 240C), which was new as a Green Line coach to Romford. It later became a coverable open-topper for the London tour and in 2001 passed to the Wells & Young brewery in Bedford. It is seen here in 2010.

Another mobile bar to appear at the event, in 2012, was DAF SB220 G134 CLF with a converted Hispano Carracera body. Having been new to TIBS in Singapore, it also saw service with operators in the UK, the most notable perhaps being Swanbrooks Travel of Cheltenham.

St John Ambulance has a presence at many major events across the UK, Showbus being no exception. In 2008, Optare-bodied DAF SB200 G253 EHD was a working part of the event, having been new to Wall of Fallowfield as a single-door forty-nine-seater.

London Country took the largest fleet of new Leyland Nationals, totalling over 540. Most of these were the 10.3-metre SNB/C classes. However, the first seventy were the longer 11.3-metre version, including LN7 (NPD 107L), which had been converted into a sales unit in 1979, a guise it lasted in until sold for scrap in 1989. It is seen here in 1984.

It's hard now to believe that when Showbus 1982 took place at Woburn, Leyland Nationals were still being built. The following year sees dual-doored Crossville SNG14 (MTU 14Y) with the revised livery for the Runcorn Busway at Woburn.

Following customer feedback, Leyland introduced a suburban coach version of the National with improved seating that was more suited for longer journeys than pure urban routes. Several NBC fleets used them on longer routes, including Hants & Dorset, where 3641 (GLJ 677N) was new in 1975. It is seen here in 2004.

Leyland-built RRM 148M was a demonstration vehicle with a higher level flat floor under the 'Suburban Express' branding. With the exception of forward-facing seats and better views out of the windows in the forward section, it had few advantages. It is seen here in 2012.

Leyland had updated the National in 1980. Gone was the 510 engine and in its place was the choice of the Leyland 0.680 or the Gardner 6HLX series or, as fitted to LFR 860X, the TL11 unit that had superseded the 0.680. Although a Cumberland vehicle, it was on loan to United Counties in 1992 when it attended Showbus.

Stagecoach operated two Leyland DAB artics in the late 1980s that had been new to SYPTE, although they were acquired from McGills of Barrhead. Allocated to the Winchester depot of the former Hampshire Bus subsidiary, FHE 291V has made the trip to the 1988 event. Of note is the use of mustard instead of orange for the top stripe, as the original livery in Scotland was applied.

BX07 NMF had made the long trip from Manchester Airport in 2010. It was one of a pair purchased new in 2007 with much additional luggage space, allowing for only forty-one seats to be fitted, hidden by the considerable amount of contravision. Boosted by London sales, the Citaro was the top-selling bendy-bus in the UK by a considerable margin.

Morton's impressed at the 2012 event with H15 BUS, which had been new in 1994 to Citybus Belfast as 3001 (DAZ 3001). The Van Hool seventy-nine-seat body is mounted on a Volvo B10M-55 chassis. A twist of fate would later take the bendy back to Belfast with Allen's Tours.

Ensignbus entered P563 MSX for the 2014 event, one of a batch of Volvo B10M Plaxton artics that had been new to Stagecoach for Express work in 1996/7. This one was initially used on services from Fife to Glasgow, where it's seventy-one-seat capacity was helpful at peak times.

United Counties were a joint founder in 1934 of the Associated Motorways pool of services between the Midlands and the south and west of England, with a hub at Cheltenham. Wearing a reversal of the bus livery for its share of the network is CNH 862, a Bristol LWL6B with a thirty-three-seat rear-entrance ECW body of 1952. It is seen here in 2007.

Fronted by two display boards that help tell its life story, preserved ex-Eastern National Bristol MW6G 573 UVX is seen at Woburn in 1989. It was one of five that had been new in 1961 for extended tours and the ECW body was fitted with thirty-four seats against forty-five for a bus-seated version. Of note also are the single-leaf door and hinged opening driver's windscreen.

Royal Blue was a long-established name in express coaching to the South West. Typical of its intake during the mid-1950s was Bristol LS6G ECW 1299 (OTT 98), complete with a roof-mounted luggage space that would be needed for the thirty-nine potential passengers' holiday bags. It is seen here in 1989.

New to Lincolnshire, 2609 (OFW 806) was a Bristol SC4LK with ECW C33F body from 1957. It is arriving through the deer park at the 1987 Showbus event. The county being very flat, with the exception of Lincoln, allowed the operator to specify smaller engines, with the four-cylinder LK considered adequate for all SCs.

The main customers for the Bristol RE/ECW combination were companies that later became part of the National Bus Company. It would be deregulation in 1986 that would see many operated by companies in competition with their former owners. RAH 681F had been new in 1967 to Eastern Counties before transfer to Cambus, then on to Milton Keynes Citybus before heading to Busways in Tyne & Wear in 1994. It would later be preserved and is seen here in 1996.

Royal Blue's parent Western National and Southern National were part of the Tilling group, which led to the purchase of Bristol/ECW vehicles for the fleet, as shown by 1472 (RDV 423H), a 1970 Bristol RELH6G with ECW body painted in the initial National livery. It is seen leaving the 1984 Showbus event.

Most NBC fleets were to standardise on the Bristol RE. With the RELH's higher chassis, underfloor lockers and a small boot were fitted, making them ideal for both service work and express work. New to United, 6080 (SNH 80L) carried the first version of the National livery, as seen at Duxford in 2009. From the mid-1970s the Leopard became the main choice for National coaches.

Eastern National VHK 177L was chosen to be rebuilt in 1981 as a prototype for ECW's B51 coach body for NBC. Whilst the production run was on Leyland Leopard or Tiger chassis, this was a Bristol RELH6G, which prevented the rear body droop that occurred on the tailless Leyland chassis and would plague the design. By 2008 it was in preservation.

In 2005 the two prototype Bristol LS are seen posed with Concorde 101 G-AXDN standing over them. 2800 (NHU 2) was an LSX6B model with a forty-two-seat dual-door body for Bristol Omnibus, whereas LL744 (MAH 744) was an LSX4G with a single-door forty-two-seat body for Eastern Counties.

Showbus often produces line-ups that cannot be repeated elsewhere, but perhaps Lincolnshire 2378 (OVL 473), a 1960 Bristol FS5G, and Eastern Counties LFL57 (557 BNG), a rare Bristol FL5G with H37/33R bodywork, may have met as the companies met at several locations around the Wash estuary. This is Showbus 1997.

Until the 1960s many operators opted for the rebodied option on mid-life chassis. BRM 596, a Leyland TD4, had been new in 1935 with a Massey body to Cumberland. In 1950 it was sent to Lowestoft, where ECW fitted a replacement body. Withdrawn in 1959, it then saw service until 1965 with Barton of Chilwell, from whom it was acquired for preservation. It is seen here in 1998.

Wearing the Tilling green of Hants & Dorset, 1568 (LEL 652F), a Bristol AVW-engined FLF, arrives at Woburn in 1987. Although preserved at the time, this particular bus was exported to Holland in the 1990s and would later be fitted with a DAF engine.

Having started life as Crosville's 811 DFM, this Bristol MW6G with ECW body later became recovery vehicle G341 in 1958 when its passenger-carrying days were over. It is seen here in 2012. The company had several of these conversions across its vast empire and they usually ran on trade plates when required.

New to Eastern Counties in 1963 as a sixty-seater bus, LFS49 (49 CNG), a Bristol FS5G, had been converted in the mid-1970s to recovery vehicle X56 and passed to Cambus in 1984. It is seen here in 1987. When it was sold, the registration remained with Cambus and was later used on several coaches.

One of the few new buses delivered during the Second World War was GHT 127, a Bristol K5G with ECW bodywork that was allocated to Bristol Omnibus, who later converted it to open-top for seasonal use. By 1990 Badgerline were using it on the Bath sightseeing tour for Guide Friday.

Departing Showbus 1989 into the setting sun, this is LEV 917, a Leyland PD1 with Alexander bodywork that had been new to City Coaches of Brentwood as its LD1 in 1947. By 1952 City had been taken over by Eastern National, where the conversion to open-top was made in 1958 for use at Southend.

For the summer season of 1961 Devon General purchased nine convertible open-top Leyland Atlanteans with Metro-Cammell bodywork, DL925–33 (925–33 GTA). All had famous naval-themed names, earning the class the nickname of Sea-Dogs. 932 GTA was also to work for East Yorkshire before being sold for preservation and is seen here in 1992.

Arriving at Showbus 1985, this is Hastings & District's HKL 836, one of a trio of Beadle-bodied AEC Regals that had been new in 1947 to Maidstone & District. In the late 1950s they were converted to open-top for the Hastings seafront service. Later passing through various hands, all three of these attractive thirty-five-seaters are still around.

As well as the major tourist spots, City Sightseeing have tried tours in other locations, sometimes seasonal only and requiring just one bus. Ipswich Transport Atlantean 9 (MRT 9P) was one of a batch of five similar Roe-bodied examples delivered in 1976. It's an early arrival at a damp Duxford in 2004.

One of the thirty Atlanteans diverted from Midland Red to London Country, AN110 (MPJ 210L) was initially allocated to Luton to replace RTs. By 1982 it had been converted to open-top for the London Tour. On the split of London Country in 1986 it was at Harlow and was later repainted into the new North East colours, as seen at the 1990 event.

Above and below: Two of Leyland's top-end Royal Tigers with Roe bodywork arrive at Showbus 1984. Crosville's CYL429 (429 UFM) was one of a pair that had their registrations transferred from Bristol MWs, while the Eastern Scottish example carries XL563 (A563 BSX), being a regular performer on the Edinburgh–London route. With a production run of six years between 1982 and 1988, only about 180 underframes were built, of which just over half carried this style of bodywork, while the rest were bodied by Van Hool or Plaxton. It became the last new coach chassis produced by Leyland.

Yelloway had been an operator of express coaches from Manchester for many years. From 1961 the company were loyal to the AEC Reliance, such as YDK 590, one of five taken in 1961 with the Harrington Cavalier bodies that would be the preferred body choice until the closure of Harrington in 1966, when Yelloway switched to Plaxton bodies. It is seen here in 1988.

Also new in 1961 was PCK 618, one of twenty Leyland L2s that had Harrington Cavalier bodies, which was configured with thirty-two reclining seats for extended tours for Ribble Motor Services. It is seen here in 2009. Uniquely, this batch were also fitted with air suspension, a feature that was not repeated. Like many tour coaches of the era, they were put into store through the winter.

Showing that the Arriva name crosses into mainland Europe, 2006 saw the appearance of 8080 (BS-DZ-51), a Scania N94UA that had come across from the Arriva Netherlands fleet for the event, adding an international tag to Showbus.

New in 1954 to Lisbon Electric Tramways, GB-21-07 was an AEC Regent III with Weymann body that later returned to the UK for preservation. Although many UK-built half-cabs were exported, they seem a little strange. Now registered in the UK as KSV 102, it's seen arriving at the final Duxford event in 2014.

For many years the CIE fleet had been loyal to Leyland for almost all its new vehicles, including a number of 12-metre Leopards such as M177 (177 IK), for which the operator built the body. Like many of the class, a DAF engine was fitted in later life. It is seen here in 2015.

New to Sheffield in 1973, Roe-bodied Atlantean UWA 312L had been exported to Australia and finished its days near Sydney as a fake London bus for use on the Blue Mountains tour. It returned to the UK in 2011 and was entered at the 2012 event.

The MD class had a short working life in the capital, only lasting seven years, MD73 (KJD 273P) being no exception. After spending two years stored, it was sold to a Swedish owner, who took it home in 1985, returning to the 1991 event with Swedish registration BNZ-019.

Stagecoach secured a large batch of former Citybus (Hong Kong) Alexander RH-bodied Olympians in the early 2000s for use on its recently introduced Megabus operation. When new vehicles arrived, many were then cascaded to other duties. 13640 (G283 YRJ) had become part of a rail replacement fleet for South West Trains when seen in 2006.

One of 152 Bristol RELL6L chassis that had been exported in kit form during the 1970s to Christchurch, New Zealand, for bodying locally. Bayline on the North Island purchased many when Christchurch had withdrawn them, including JD 4954, which was returned to the UK for preservation in 2011, where it became XOU 936T. It is seen here in 2014.

The thirty Dragons with Met-Sec bodies that Stagecoach had operated in Kenya were returned to work for the group in the UK, after which many were seen as good investments for school duties. M682 TDB was one of three operated by Landmark Travel of Arlesey in Bedfordshire and is seen here in 2014.

Woburn 2015 produced an impressive display of Britain's oldest buses, with around a dozen entered that were built before the Second World War. Several, including LF 8375, a 1911 AEC B-type with London General body, dated from before the First World War. New to General as B1609, it's seen between Woburn village and the abbey.

Part of the fantastic selection of old Leylands owned locally in Mike Sutcliffe's private collection, LN 7270 dated from 1908. A Leyland X2 with a Tilling body seating thirty-four, it had been new to London Central as its No. 14.

Also from the Mike Sutcliffe collection was BD 209, a 1921 Leyland G7 with thirty-two-seat Dobson body that had been new to United Counties as B15. Two more of the collection can be seen in the background: C 2367, a Leyland G new to Todmorden in 1931, is to the left and HE 12, a 1913 Leyland S that had been new to Barnsley & District, is to the right.

New in 1920, this Albion A16 charabanc was initially owned by the New Zealand government. The chassis was repatriated in the early 2000s and rebuilt with a replica body. The registration BF 7455 was obtained for the completed vehicle, which needed a lift to the abbey for the event in 2015.

First Manchester F288 DRJ has made the long trip south in 2003. New to Greater Manchester, this Northern Counties-bodied Olympian wears the former Bolton livery. First have painted quite a few vehicles in traditional liveries over the years.

An early arrival at the 2006 event was Volvo Olympian 16221 (R701 DNH) of Stagecoach in Bedford, wearing the Tilling-style livery of the 1950s and 1960s on its Alexander RL body. A nice touch was the 'blue of Bedford' fleet number plates that were also fitted.

Seen under a very grey sky in 1990 is this Midland Red (South) Leyland Olympian/ ECW (C964 XVC), which had been painted into the former Stratford Blue livery. Around the late 1980s the former Midland Red fleets had few double-deckers.

Later to become part of the Stagecoach heritage fleet, Bristol VRT/ECW 5030 (JOU 160P) appeared at the 1989 event in traditional Cheltenham Tramways livery for their Diamond Jubilee in 1989. Originally built as a dual-door bus, it was converted to single-door, but the centre stairs gave the game away for those in the know.

WLT 916 had started life as Yorkshire Coastline P426 WUG, one of a batch of Alexander Royale Volvo Olympians. They were retained by Ensignbus for both service and contract work, including rail replacements around London and sometimes well beyond. It's seen at the 2011 event alongside RT8 (FXT 183), which Ensignbus retained in their heritage fleet.

Many of the TL class of London Country ECW-bodied Tigers were rebodied in the early 1990s with East Lancs bodies. TL39 (WPH 139Y) became part of the Ensignbus Stratford Blue operation, which had been acquired from Guide Friday. Later entering preservation, it appeared at the 2009 event in Midland Red colours but is seen here in 2002.

Former East Kent MFN 946F, an AEC Regent V with Park Royal body, had been acquired by Hastings & District and repainted into their privatisation livery when seen in 1990. With Hastings and East Kent both acquired by Stagecoach, it would later reappear in the heritage fleet in its former glory as a traditional East Kent-liveried vehicle.

While Stagecoach was fairly happy with the Olympian for its double-deck needs, what was on offer for full-sized single-deck replacements was a bit limited. Cumberland had taken a few Lynxes so perhaps it was a bit of a surprise when Hampshire Bus took a trio of Dennis Javelins with Duple 300 bodies. New as 802, F136 SPX arrives at Woburn in 1989.

In 1989 Western Travel had taken a batch of five Leyland Olympians, with Alexander
RL bodies, to an almost Stagecoach configuration for its Swindon operation, including
101 (G101 AAD), seen at the 1994 event at Duxford. By a strange twist of fate, Stagecoach
had purchased the Western Travel business the previous December and these buses would
later receive group colours.

Very few Leyland Swifts operated in the Stagecoach Group. Reeve Burgess-bodied
H201 XKH had arrived with the purchase of Cleveland Transit in 1994, having been new to
York Pullman before seeing service with Hull. It is seen here attending the 1996 event.

When new, N450 XVA, a Volvo B10M/Plaxton Expressliner, had been allocated to Premier Travel's Cambridge–London NX Shuttle. Like many Stagecoach vehicles, however, cascades as new rolling stock arrived had seen a move across to the former Red & White fleet. It is seen here in 2005.

Stagecoach acquired the operations of Cavalier of Long Sutton in 2008, which formed the basis of the Fens fleet. The newest vehicle in the fleet, 21217 (KT57 MTE), a Volvo B7RLE with Wright body, was quickly repainted into group colours but its stay was brief, being a leased vehicle. A second appearance, though, at the 2010 event, was made while owned by Midland Classic.

Over the years, numerous Bedford OBs have appeared at the event. The 2011 appearance of LTA 752 did turn a few heads after Lodges Coaches had rebuilt it with removable windows for use on special events, to give a true vintage appeal.

Black & White had taken thirty-eight Daimler Roadliners with Plaxton bodies between 1967 and 1970. 316 (UAD 316H) was one of the last batch of ten delivered with Perkins engines. All were sold on after short working lives. In this 1989 shot at Woburn, it's in Offerton Coaches of Stockport livery, although it was owned by Knotty Bus.

Based at Porton Down on Salisbury Plain, Silver Star ran many express services across the country for servicemen on weekend leave to get back home. MMR 553 was a Leyland Tiger Cub with a Harrington body of 1955. The ending of National Service in the early 1960s heralded the beginning of the company's demise; it was sold in 1963 to Wilts & Dorset and is seen here in 2007.

New in May 1970, this Alexander Y type-bodied Leopard would only be part of the Stratford Blue fleet until January 1971, when the business passed to Midland Red. 36 (XNX 136H) would become 2036 with its new owners and, on the split of Midland Red in 1981, would form part of the Midland Red North fleet. It is seen here in 1989.

The North Western name was revised by NBC, on the split of Ribble in 1986, for operations around Merseyside. Acquired by Drawline in 1988, they soon took new vehicles, mainly Dennis chassis with East Lancs bodywork. This combination is seen on 635 (F635 BKD), a recently delivered Dominator, at the 1989 event in the company's distinctive livery.

Eastern Counties adopted this livery to replace NBC red in the mid-1980s and it would last until Badgerline colours took over. DD2 (F102 AVG) was one of a batch of five Leyland Olympians with Northern Counties bodies supplied in 1989; these were their first new double-deckers for many years.

East Kent was much admired in the pre-NBC days for its smartly turned out fleet of mostly AEC and Leyland buses. However, after its management buyout, the company turned to MCW for its new double-deckers and, after the demise of MCW in 1989, the company returned to Leyland for ten Olympians with Northern Counties bodies in 1990, such as 7806 (H806 BKK), seen soon after delivery.

Potteries had taken a batch of ten Leyland-bodied Olympians shortly before the 1989 event. Seven of these, including 757 (G757 XRE), were route branded for the 320 route. They also featured coach seats. At this time, the company was management-owned, but it later sold out to Badgerline.

Although ordered by the old North Western company, twenty-five Bristol VRT/ECWs were delivered to SELNEC in 1972. They were withdrawn mid-life as non-standard and many passed to other operators for further service, such as former 421 (AJA 421J), which by 1986 had become part of the Stevensons fleet.

South Yorkshire PTE amassed a large fleet of Metrobuses which included some in its 'Fastline' livery for limited stop routes across its network. 1950 (C950 HWF) shows the red blinds used for these routes, as well as the high-backed seats, as it arrives at Woburn in 1985.

West Midlands opted for Scania N113DRBs with Alexander RH bodywork for a forty-vehicle order in 1990. They were numbered between 3201 and 3247; there were gaps as the DVLA had started selective issue of registration plates and 205/13/14/16/22/30/40 fell into this category and were not used. H223 LOM is seen in 2003, by now owned locally by Alec Head.

West Midlands PTE had upset many local councillors in the mid-1970s by ordering Scottish-built Volvo Ailsas instead of Fleetlines, which were made locally. In the end fifty-three Ailsas with Alexander AV bodywork were purchased, but in a strange twist of fate most were sold to London on deregulation. 4766 (JOV 466P) is seen screaming through the deer park at Woburn in 1984.

Delivered as new to London General in 1993, VN8 (K8 KLL) was a Northern Counties Volvo B10B. It moved to Oxford Bus in 1997, becoming K125 BUD. By 2010 it was with Southern Vectis and had been converted, as seen here in 2011, for use on a circular route in Shanklin.

In 1985 the minibus revolution was in full swing, bringing several of the type to Showbus. TR 6170 was perhaps the most unusual small vehicle present, a 5/8 scale Lion omnibus that had been built in 1972 and which, despite its size, was able to carry eight passengers.

Local operator Dews provided a varied line-up in 2009, with former Black Prince Leyland Titan PTF 702F flanked by two very different single-deckers. The Dart carries a very apt registration as it was used on service to the city of Ely.

An unusual Optare Solo at the 2009 event, YJ56 AOV was owned by St Dunstan's for use transporting blind veterans on holidays to their home at Brighton. The 10.2-metre vehicle was fitted with thirty-three coach seats. Like many Solos, it carries Yorkshire plates.

Between 1953 and 1955, Trent took twenty-one Leyland Titan PD2/12s with Leyland-built bodies. 1256 (FRC 956) was the final member of the last batch, and also the final Leyland-built body of that generation, although production of front-engine Titans would continue for another decade. It is seen here in 1989.

The development of the rear-engine bus in the late 1950s was perhaps one of the biggest changes in the industry. Walsall Corporation took the shortest Fleetlines built at a mere 27 feet 6 inches, and the largest at 36 feet in 1968 with the arrival of 56 (XDH 56G). As well as the dual doors, two staircases were fitted with the Cummins V6 engine fitted in the rear offside corner, allowing seating for eighty-six. It would later become part of the West Midlands PTE fleet and is seen here in 2015.

Derby were one of many operators that switched from Leyland products during the 1980s, and in 1984 they received a batch of ten Volvo B10Ms with Marshall bodies. The first of the batch, 134 (B134 GAU), passes Woburn church in 1989. The employee buy-out of the company was helped by backing from the local Luton & District company, who had become the first such company in 1987. Only fifteen B10M double-deckers were bodied by Marshall, of which Derby took thirteen.

Rhymney Valley had taken a batch of three Leyland Olympians with East Lancs bodies in 1985. All were disposed of after a couple of years. C29 EUH had become Badgerline 5001 when seen at the 1989 event in a non-standard livery. When new, all three had carried Inter Valley Link livery.

The final event at Duxford in 2014 saw a BBC film unit on site for the event, with Dom Littlewood. Later it was shown on BBC TV's *One Show* as part of a feature on concessionary bus passes for the over-sixties. Here, Dom Littlewood can be seen in the cab of former Birmingham Leyland PS1/Weymann JOJ 245.

Rally plaques are often fitted to those vehicles that attend the event, they but usually disappear off in service vehicles shortly afterwards. So it came as a surprise to find that the plaque for the first Duxford event was still fitted to Megadekka 14000 (F110 NES) of Stagecoach at the 2012 event, and at the time of writing (2019) was still fitted.